David Rice Whitney

The Suffolk Bank

David Rice Whitney

The Suffolk Bank

ISBN/EAN: 9783337242589

Printed in Europe, USA, Canada, Australia, Japan

Cover: Foto ©Suzi / pixelio.de

More available books at **www.hansebooks.com**

THE

SUFFOLK BANK.

BY

D. R. WHITNEY,

PRESIDENT OF THE SUFFOLK NATIONAL BANK.

" *Othello's occupation 's gone.*"

MOOR OF VENICE, Act III., Scene 3.

CAMBRIDGE:

𝕻rinted at the 𝕽iverside 𝕻ress

FOR PRIVATE DISTRIBUTION.

1878.

To

JOHN AMORY LOWELL, LL. D.,

ONE OF THE ORIGINATORS OF

THE SUFFOLK BANK SYSTEM,

WHO SERVED ON THE FOREIGN MONEY COMMITTEE

DURING THE WHOLE OF ITS EXISTENCE,

This Sketch of the History of the Suffolk Bank

IS

RESPECTFULLY INSCRIBED.

PREFACE.

The following sketch was written with no intention of entering into a vindication of the Suffolk Bank System. The benefits conferred upon the currency of New England by the Suffolk Bank are now universally acknowledged; the ill feelings against it, arising sometimes from personal but oftener from pecuniary considerations, have long since passed away; and the incorporation of its system of redemption into the present National Bank Act shows that its fundamental principle, that a bank currency to be sound must be redeemable on demand, still survives.

Its object is to place on record a concise history of the bank, and to give the credit of inaugurating and sustaining its foreign money system of redemption to those to whom it justly belongs: the reputation of which has sometimes been claimed for those in no way entitled to it.

The materials for this sketch have been collected almost entirely from the records of the bank, to which, as one of the officers of the Suffolk National Bank, I have had free access: and it is printed in accordance with a request made by the present Board of Directors of that bank. D. R. W.

Boston, *January* 1, 1878.

CONTENTS

—— ·——

CHAPTER I.

1818.

CHAPTER IV.

1837–1842.

CHAPTER V.

1842–1853.

CHAPTER VI.

1853–1857.

CHAPTER VII.

1855–1866.

CHAPTER VIII.

1865–1878.

APPENDIX.

THE SUFFOLK BANK.

CHAPTER I.

THE business man of to-day knows little by experience of the inconvenience and loss suffered by the merchant of sixty years ago, arising from the currency in which debts were then paid. The national bank-notes which he now receives are current for their face value, whether issued by the National Bank of Commerce of New York, with a capital of five million dollars, or by the National Bank of Yankton, Dakota, with a capital of fifty thousand. Each is alike secured by the pledge of the faith of the whole people of the United States. He cares not by what national banks the notes are issued, where they may be situated, whether they are sound or whether they are insolvent. He receives them to-day in payment at their face, knowing that to-morrow he can use them in any State of the Union, California alone excepted, without possibility of loss either from depreciation or lack of currency. Not so with the merchant of 1818. Receiving payment in bank-notes, he assorted them into two parcels, current and uncurrent. In the first he placed the notes issued by the solvent banks of his own city; in the other the bills of all

1

other banks. Upon these latter there was a discount, varying in amount according to the location and the credit of the bank issuing them. How great the discount was he could learn only by consulting his "Bank Note Reporter," or by inquiring at the nearest exchange office; and he could avail himself of them only by selling them to a dealer in uncurrent money. He could neither deposit them, nor use them in payment of his notes at a bank. The discount on them varied from one per cent. upwards, according to the distance the bills had to be sent for redemption and the financial standing of the bank by which they were issued. (Many banks were established in remote places, mainly for the purpose of making a profit on circulation. The more distant they were from the business centres the more expensive it was to send their bills home for redemption, and the more difficult it was for the general public to know their true financial condition.

This unsatisfactory state of the currency, with its annoyances and risks, continued till the establishment of the Suffolk Bank system, so called, in 1824,—a system of redemption identical with, and which served as a model for, the present National Redemption Agency at Washington.)

On the twenty-seventh of February, 1818, an institution was organized which was destined to exert upon the currency of New England an influence little dreamed of by its projectors, but so wholesome that it gave uniformity and stability to the circulation, reduced the discount on it to a minimum, and by holding it in check tended to keep it in a sound and healthy condition.) On that day a company of mer-

chants and others met at the Exchange Coffee House
in Boston, a then noted tavern situated near State
Street, for the purpose of organizing under a charter,
just obtained from the Legislature of Massachusetts,
for a new bank, to be called the Suffolk. The charter
was granted on the tenth of February, 1818, to Samuel
R. Miller, Patrick T. Jackson, Eliphalet Williams, William Lawrence, Daniel P. Parker, George Bond, Edmund Munroe, and their associates, and was to continue till the first of October, 1831.

The total number of banks then in operation in
Boston was six, namely, the Massachusetts, Union, Boston, State, New England, and Manufacturers and Mechanics', afterwards changed to the Tremont.

The State Bank had been chartered in 1811, seven
years previous, and the charter of the Suffolk Bank
was granted subject to the same restrictions and taxes
and entitled to the same privileges as the State Bank.
By it the usual powers of receiving money on deposit,
loaning the same, buying and selling specie and bills
of exchange, and issuing its own notes, were granted
to the new bank. The capital was fixed at $500,000.
The liabilities, exclusive of sums due on account of
deposits, were limited in debts by bond, bill, note, or
other contract to twice the amount of its capital, and
the loans were subject to the same limitation, the
directors being liable for any excess.

For the privileges granted by this charter the State
was at liberty to subscribe for an increase of stock
equal to one half of the paid-up capital, to appoint a
pro rata proportion of directors, and to borrow at any
one time it might desire any sum not exceeding ten
per cent. of the capital of the bank, payable at any

time short of five years, at five per cent. interest; and its total liability to the bank was limited to twenty per cent. of the capital.

The bank was also required to appropriate one tenth of its whole funds to loan to citizens of the Commonwealth, residing out of Boston, engaged in agriculture or manufactures, in sums not less than one hundred or over five hundred dollars, with interest annually, these loans to be secured by mortgage.

The stockholders were liable in a sum equal to the amount of stock held by them for losses arising from the mismanagement of the directors; and were also liable, proportionately, for the redemption of the bills at the expiration of the charter. The tax was fixed at one half of one per cent. on the capital.

Among the subscribers to the stock were many of the most influential men of the day. The original subscription list is as follows: —

	NUMBER OF SHARES.		NUMBER OF SHARES.
William Appleton	50	French & Tucker	50
Nathan Appleton	300	Thaddeus Fiske	20
Timothy Bigelow	10	Gardiner Green	230
Charles Barnard	16	Henry Hubbard	50
Eben. and John Breed	100	Augustine Heard	50
Thomas Brewer	30	Samuel Hubbard	100
John W. Boott	200	Barnabas Hedge	50
Josiah Bradlee	120	William Hammatt	20
John Brooks	10	Robert & John Hooper	50
Buffington & Thomas	40	Patrick T. Jackson	300
Nathan Bridge & Co.	100	Charles Lowell	15
Bordman & Pope	100	Caleb Loring	100
Joseph Chapin	5	A. & A. Lawrence	50
John Cunningham	50	Luther Lawrence	25
Pickering Dodge	50	William Lawrence	300
Otis Everett	50	Lunt & Leech	40
Ebenezer Francis	300	Israel Munson	184
Jeremiah Fitch & Co.	20	Thos. & Edw. Motley	50

Number of Shares.		Number of Shares.	
Perrin May	50	Henry G. Rice	30
Edmund Munroe	300	John T. Reed	30
Marblehead Marine Insur-		W. S. Rogers	50
ance Co.	100	Benjamin Seaver	5
William Pratt	20	Henry H. Tuckerman	25
William Prescott	50	Upham & Faulkner	50
William Payne	200	Alfred Welles	50
Daniel P. Parker	300	S. G. Williams & Co.	100
Dudley L. Pickman	50	Eliphalet Williams	50
Jeffrey Richardson	25	John Wood	50
Andrew Ritchie	50	Williams & Wood	100
Nathaniel P. Russell	50	Samuel K. Williams	30

A Board of Directors was at once chosen, and authorized to draw up a code of by-laws for the government of the new bank, engage suitable rooms for its business, and do all such other things as were necessary to put it in successful operation.

The first directors were Ebenezer Breed, Andrew Ritchie, Thomas Motley, Samuel Hubbard, John W. Boott, George Bond, Daniel P. Parker, William Lawrence, Eliphalet Williams, Edmund Munroe, Patrick T. Jackson and Ebenezer Francis, who met· from time to time at the Exchange Coffee House, till the nineteenth of March, when they adjourned to rooms hired temporarily, on the second floor of the building on State Street owned by Mr. Barney Smith, and here the bank opened for business on the first of April, 1818, — Ebenezer Francis having been in the mean time elected President, and Matthew S. Parker Cashier. These premises were occupied thirteen months. On the seventeenth of April, 1819, the bank was moved to rooms on the second floor of the building on the corner of State and Kilby streets, then and now occupied in part by the New England Bank.

The directors at once, in addition to the regular business of discounting commercial paper, turned their attention to foreign exchange ; and on the fifteenth of August, 1818, appointed a committee to obtain a loan by the issue of post-notes, and to purchase exchange on London with the proceeds. This exchange was remitted to Messrs. J. & S. Nicholson, Jansen & Co., of London, and the bank sold its own bills drawn against the same. On the twelfth of September a vote was passed, holding the capital of the bank responsible to its London agents for any overdraft. To the business of buying and selling exchange was added that of buying in London United States stock and dollars. The foreign exchange business was continued till April, 1826, when a final settlement was made with Messrs. Brown, Jansen & Co., the London agents, and the bank turned its attention almost exclusively to receiving and redeeming the bills issued by the New England banks. During this period the bank paid its stockholders an average dividend of five and one half per cent. per annum ; its largest dividend was seven per cent. and its smallest five per cent. per annum.

CHAPTER II.

THE first Board of Directors were active, energetic men, and strove to keep the bank abreast of the times. In addition to the foreign exchange business they saw that they might add to the profits of the bank by buying country bank-notes at a discount and sending them home for redemption. The only bank then doing this business was the New England. Accordingly, on the seventeenth of February, 1819, a committee was appointed to take into consideration the subject of foreign money, and report at the next meeting. By the term "foreign money" was meant, not the money of foreign countries, but the notes issued by banks outside of Boston. It will be necessary for a clear understanding of what follows to keep this distinction in mind. The committee consisted of the President and Messrs. Appleton and Breed; and on the twenty-fourth of February it reported, "That it is expedient to receive at the Suffolk Bank the several kinds of foreign money which are now received at the New England Bank, and at the same rates. That if any bank will deposit with the Suffolk Bank five thousand dollars as a permanent deposit, with such further sums as shall be sufficient from time to time to redeem its bills taken by this bank, such bank shall have the privilege of receiving its own bills at the same discount at which they are purchased." They further recommend "That the banks located in Providence and Newport," and twenty-three other banks then keeping an account with the Suffolk, "shall have the privilege of receiving such of their bills as may be received by the Suffolk Bank at the same discount as taken, without the permanent deposit of five thousand dollars, provided said banks will make *all* their deposits at the Suffolk Bank, and at all times have money sufficient to redeem the bills taken." Also, "That should any bank refuse to make the deposit required, the bills of such banks shall be sent home for payment at such times and in such manner as the directors may hereafter order and direct.")

This vote and the action proceeding from it, coupled with the energy of the President, resulted in an extensive business. Buying and selling exchange had heretofore been conducted by a committee, consisting of the President and Messrs. Breed and Belknap. To this committee authority was given to purchase at a discount the bills of banks outside of Boston and send them home for specie.) At the same time a vote was passed, authorizing the President to compound with any bank not to purchase its bills. With the New England Bank the Suffolk at once entered into a lively competition; and, as a natural consequence, the discount on country bank-notes was materially lessened. Previous to this time the discount on Massachusetts bills had been one per cent., and on the bills of other States much greater. Competition at once reduced the rate on the former to one half of one per cent., and even lower.) In 1822, the profits on the business had become so small that the directors felt obliged to reduce the expenses of the bank; which they did by abolishing the office of discount clerk, and appointing the President "a committee to inquire if any further saving in the expenses of the bank can be made."

(The animosity of the country banks which were unwilling to keep a deposit in Boston for the redemption of their bills was naturally very much aroused when the Suffolk Bank, collecting their bills, sent them home for specie; and much ill-feeling was engendered.)

On one occasion, early in 1824, the Suffolk Bank sent a messenger to a bank in Springfield, with $22,600 of its bills, with orders to present them for payment in specie. The bank could not respond; and after much delay the messenger agreed to take in part payment a draft on Boston for $5,000, — at a discount of three eighths of one per cent. This draft was duly presented and payment received. On the same day one of the members of the firm upon whom the draft was drawn, and who were the Boston agents of the country bank, called upon the cashier of the Suffolk, and asked him how much discount had been taken upon the draft that day paid. The cashier replied, three eighths of one per cent. Whereupon the gentleman, in the excitement of the moment, applied some very abusive remarks to the President. These remarks were reported to the Board of Directors by the cashier; and by the board referred to a committee, who at once entered into a correspondence with the gentleman upon the subject. He apologized for the use of the abusive language, saying he had no recollection of the words themselves, and, in so far as they were abusive, he wholly disapproved and condemned them; but would make no other apology satisfactory to the board, or change his opinion of the action of

2

the bank in its transaction with the country bank for which his firm acted as agents.

The directors, in vindication of themselves, sent a copy of the whole correspondence to each of the Boston banks. ⟨A single quotation will show the position they took ; what they believed to be their rights ; and the principles by which they were guided. They write : —

"The directors think it unnecessary to make any remark upon the right which one corporation has to demand of another the payment of its just debts ; and in their banking operations they not only profess, but intend, to be governed by those wholesome rules and regulations which are for the mutual good of all banking institutions."

This right, thus early enunciated, was that upon which the whole Suffolk Bank system was founded ; upon it the bank rested during the whole existence of the system ; and in giving it up forty years later the directors placed upon record this, among other reasons, " because the right to demand specie of a bank for its promise to pay cannot be given up without destroying the efficacy of the system."

An effort was made seven years afterwards to have the account of the transaction expunged from the records of the bank, but without success. It remains there to this day, in evidence of the deep feeling existing against the Suffolk Bank for exercising a right, the justice of which no one can question.

⟨At this time the city was flooded with country money. The circulation consisted almost entirely of the notes of banks outside of Boston. With more than one half of the banking capital of New England, the Boston banks supplied only one twenty-fifth of the bills in use.⟩ Two of the directors of the Suffolk

Bank, Messrs. John A. Lowell and William Lawrence, both actively engaged in the distribution of textile fabrics throughout New England, had become deeply impressed with the evils attending this undue issue of country money. They had experienced these evils not only in their own business, but, as directors in the bank, they had seen how small a proportion of the circulation was enjoyed by the city banks. They had given so much consideration to the subject, and were so deeply interested in it, that they were appointed by the Suffolk Bank a committee, for the purpose of conferring with the other banking institutions of the city concerning the measures which it might be expedient for them in common to adopt, with a view of checking the enormous issues of country, and especially Eastern, paper, and of securing to the bills of the Boston banks a just proportion of the circulation.

In accordance with the power thus conferred upon them, on the tenth of April, 1824, they addressed the following letter to each of the Boston banks : —

" The subscribers, having been chosen by the directors of the Suffolk Bank a committee for the purpose of conferring with the other banking institutions in the city concerning the measures which it might be expedient for them in common to adopt, with the view of checking the enormous issues of country, and especially Eastern, paper, and of securing to the bills of the Boston banks a just proportion of the circulation, beg leave to call the attention of your board to the following statement of facts : —

" That of the whole incorporated banking capital of New England, amounting to less than twenty million dollars, the eleven banks in this city possess ten million one hundred and fifty thousand. That estimating the circulation of the country banks at only seventy-five per cent. of their capital, which they believe to be a moderate computation, these banks furnish seven million five hundred thousand dollars of the circulating medium, while the banks in the city, with a capital equal to all the rest, keep in what may be fairly termed permanent circulation only three hundred thousand dollars. That this prodigious credit thus enjoyed by the country banks is not owing to any superior confidence in the stability of these institutions, or in their ability to redeem their promises in gold and silver, but may be attributed to a discount founded on the very difficulty and uncertainty of means of enforcing this payment. Such would not be the natural operation of these causes were these institutions what they profess to be, — establishments for the discount of country notes and the convenience of country traders. Their bills would then circulate only in their own immediate vicinity. The farmers, who come to this city to dispose of their produce, would take back Boston bills, which the traders would in their turn bring down to pay for foreign or domestic merchandise. The superior stability and security of our banks would insure this result. But under the existing circumstances we presume that a very great proportion of the discounts of the country banks are made in Boston. Loans to an immense amount are made by their agents here at reduced rates of interest, payable in three or five days after demand, so that they can be in funds at very short notice, and in this manner necessarily deprive us of much valuable business. And this great circulation is enjoyed by the banks out of the State, who do not pay the tax to the Commonwealth which we are compelled to pay. The injury to the country trade which has by some persons been apprehended from any measures which tend to curtail the issues of country paper we believe to be, in the long run, merely imaginary. No reasonable man can doubt that the banks in the interior are numerous enough for the supply of all the wants of their own traders, and the probability is, that when the time and attention of those companies shall be no longer distracted by so many negotiations foreign to their legitimate design, they will be even more liberally supplied than at present.

" The banks in New York have tried the experiment with the disadvantage of deducting no discount to reimburse them for the expense ; and yet we are assured from unquestionable authority that they find themselves amply indemnified by the increased circulation of their own city alone. We think, however, that a discount of one fourth of one per cent. would as effectually answer the end proposed, and at the same time, if judiciously managed, be nearly sufficient to pay all the attendant expense of sending home the bills even of the most distant banks.

" Since the last of January the Suffolk Bank has received nearly one million dollars of country paper, the greater part of which has been sent home for collection, or redeemed by the agents here at par. Notwithstanding the unfavorable season and bad state of the roads they do not find themselves losers by the operation. But the measures hitherto pursued have been only partially effectual. Part of the bills thus removed from circulation are replaced by a worse description of paper. The sending home of the latter must be attended with some risk, and as the benefits proposed in our increased circulation and discounts will be common to all the banks in this city, we deem it but just to call upon them to contribute their proportion towards the risk.

" With these views we make the following proposals. That a fund of ———— hundred thousand dollars, to be assessed in proportion to their respective capitals, be raised by the several banking institutions, who may agree to the arrangement, to be placed at the disposal of one or more banks for the purpose of sending home the bills of the banks in the State of Maine, in such way as may be deemed expedient. That this capital shall be paid in the bills of the several banks, which shall be indiscriminately paid out for the purchase of Eastern money. That the profit or loss shall be in common, after charging a reasonable compensation for any extra service rendered by the officers of the bank receiving them. That this fund shall be withdrawn at any time by a vote of a majority of the banks concerned, and that the president and directors of the receiving bank shall be at liberty to decline continuing the agency when they shall see fit, expecting no remuneration for the services which they may render in this business for the common good.

" The committee have no doubt that, if these measures are adopted and vigorously pursued, the banks in this place will obtain a circulation of three million dollars, and a proportionable increase in their discounts.
JOHN A. LOWELL.
WILLIAM LAWRENCE."

The consideration of this letter by the banks to which it was addressed resulted in a meeting, at which a sub-committee of one from each of the banks was appointed to take the matter into consideration. On the twenty fourth of April the sub-committee met; present, —

Mr. Head, of the Massachusetts Bank,

Mr. Freeman, of the Union Bank,

Mr. Bourne, of the State Bank,

Mr. Stevens, of the Manufacturers and Mechanics' Bank,

Mr. Williams, of the Eagle Bank,

Mr. Francis, of the Suffolk Bank ;

and it was voted, —

"That it is expedient to send home all the bank bills in circulation issued from banks out of the State, and the bills of such other banks as the committee of arrangements may think proper.

"That the sum of three hundred thousand dollars is necessary to carry the same into effect.

"That this sum should be furnished by the banks in the following proportions : —

State Bank . .	$50,000
Massachusetts Bank . . .	50,000
Union Bank	40,000
Manufacturers and Mechanics' Bank .	40,000
Columbian Bank	30,000
Eagle Bank . .	30,000
Suffolk Bank . .	60,000
	$300,000

in bills of the several banks, and paid out in equal proportions. All profits and all losses to be in proportion to the sums assessed.

"That a committee of one person be appointed from each bank concerned in the association, to be appointed by the several boards of directors of the said banks, with full powers to carry into effect the object of this meeting."

These votes were at once ratified by the banks interested ; and the Suffolk Bank was chosen to act as the agent of the associated banks.

To carry out the scheme it was agreed that the Suffolk Bank, as the agent of the associated banks, should receive from them all their foreign money at

(the same or less discount than the New England Bank,
or other banks in Boston, received it, and should send
it home for redemption ; that the associated banks
should, at all times, be ready to give advice and assistance to the Suffolk Bank in case of need ; that they
should acknowledge their interest in and support of
the measure, so long as they approved of the same ;
that if the business should be conducted in a manner
not satisfactory to any bank it might withdraw by
giving thirty days' notice ; and that the Suffolk Bank
might give up the business at any time by giving the
same notice.)

On the fifteenth of May the Suffolk Bank accepted
the agency of the association, and at once chose, as
foreign money clerks, Wm. Grubb, Jr., as principal,
with a salary of sixty dollars per month, and P. H.
White, as assistant, at fifty dollars per month. It began
the business of receiving foreign money from the associated banks under the agreement on the twenty-
fourth of May, 1824.

(The country banks naturally were very much excited, and loud in their opposition. They felt that the
result must be the curtailment of their circulation, and
the necessity of keeping a larger specie reserve. In
derision they called the associated banks the " Holy Al-
liance ;" and some dignified the Suffolk Bank with the
title of the " Six Tailed Bashaw." But they soon became convinced that a promise to pay, printed on the
face of a bank-note, meant a promise to pay specie on
demand ; that such a demand was likely to be made
upon them at any time ; and that the associated banks,
with the Suffolk as the agent, were not to be frightened
or turned out of their course by sarcastic words.)

CHAPTER III.

On the twenty-fifth of April, 1825, Mr. Ebenezer Francis, the President, resigned, and Mr. Samuel Hubbard was elected in his place. Mr. Hubbard took the office with great reluctance, only temporarily, and upon condition that a committee should be appointed to take charge of the foreign money concerns. The directors accordingly appointed, as the Foreign Money Committee, Messrs. Ebenezer Breed, William Lawrence, John A. Lowell, and Jeffrey Richardson ; and *the affairs of this department were conducted thenceforth by this committee and its successors.* Two of its original members, Messrs. John A. Lowell and Jeffrey Richardson, served during its whole existence, forty-two years; and Mr. William Lawrence served during his connection with the bank, which was dissolved by his death in 1848, twenty-three years.

Mr. Hubbard held the office of President till the following November, when he resigned; and Mr. Henry B. Stone was elected in his place. Mr. Stone was the first teller of the Suffolk Bank when it opened for business in 1818. Subsequently, and at the time of his election, he was cashier of the Eagle Bank.

On the sixteenth of May, 1825, the associated banks further agreed that the Suffolk Bank should receive from them *at par* all the country money they might receive from their depositors, and immediately

place it to the credit of the bank depositing the same.
This agreement was to be binding for sixty days; after
which any of the associated banks were at liberty to
withdraw by giving sixty days' notice. The Suffolk
Bank, however, agreed to make the agreement binding
for six, nine, or twelve months, provided the further
sum of two hundred thousand dollars should be con-
tributed by the associated banks.

By the first of November of this year the business
had increased so much that the directors voted a gratuity of seventeen hundred dollars to the clerks of the
bank for extra services. Of this amount they charged
six hundred dollars to the associated banks.

The foreign money now poured in so fast upon the
Suffolk Bank that early in December it was obliged to
make an arrangement with the associated banks to
delay drawing for their foreign money deposits as long
a time as possible; and at the same time instructions
were given to the New York agent not to purchase
any more bills of any kind in that market.

About this time the Phœnix and Pacific banks of
Nantucket failed to redeem their bills; and a special
messenger was sent to Nantucket to secure the debts
due from them. After a delay of two months a settlement was made on the following terms: The Phœnix
and Pacific banks to pay interest on their bills from the
time they were redeemed by the Suffolk Bank till demand was made, and damages at the rate of two per
cent. a month from demand till final payment. This
was the legal penalty to which banks were liable under
their charters for non-payment of their bills after due
demand made during business hours.

Early in 1826 the foreign money committee re-

3

ported that one teller, three assistant tellers, and one
messenger would be necessary to transact the business
of that department. The force was accordingly increased, and the following salaries voted, namely : first
teller, one thousand dollars per annum; first assistant,
six hundred dollars per annum ; and the second and
third assistants and messenger, five hundred dollars
each.

This year the capital of the bank was increased to.
seven hundred and fifty thousand dollars. The directors applied to the Legislature for liberty to increase the
capital to one million; but the General Court deemed
it inexpedient to grant more than one half of the
amount asked.

On the first of November, the losses in the foreign
money department had amounted to $1,183, namely :
one package of Thomaston Bank bills containing $600,
and $583 in various small deficiencies, uncurrent and
counterfeit bills. The directors, in order to reduce
the risks to a minimum, and obtain the strictest ac-
countability, entered into an agreement with Mr. Grubb,
that in consideration of $1,050 per annum, in additior.
to his regular salary, he should give bonds to indem-
nify the bank for all deficiencies, counterfeits, mutilated
or uncurrent bills in his department. He was to have
the use of three foreign money clerks, and the help of
the other clerks as heretofore ; all other help he might
require was to be at his own expense ; and the bank
was to have the right to employ the foreign money
clerks in carrying home the bills of country banks for
payment, whenever it might be necessary, without
further allowance to Mr. Grubb.

This arrangement continued eight months; when

Mr. Grubb sent the directors a communication informing them that the foreign money business had increased so much, that his compensation was not sufficient. In view of the fact that the business was in a
fair way of further increase, a new arrangement was
made with him, whereby, in consideration of $4,250
per annum, he assumed the whole expense of the foreign money department, hiring his own clerks, and
taking all risks of loss; and either party had the right
to discontinue the arrangement by giving thirty days'
notice.

(The foreign money business was now fairly established, and growing in magnitude every day. The
general arrangement made with the New England
banks, which opened an account with the Suffolk Bank
for the redemption of their bills, was as follows:
Each bank placed a permanent deposit with the Suffolk Bank of $2,000 and upwards, free of interest, the
amount depending upon the capital and business of
the bank. This sum was the minimum for banks with
a capital of $100,000 and under. In consideration of
such deposit the Suffolk Bank redeemed all the bills
of that bank which might come to it from any source,
charging the redeemed bills to the issuing bank once
a week, or whenever they amounted to a certain fixed
sum; *provided*, the bank kept a sufficient amount of
funds to its credit, independent of the permanent deposit, to redeem all of its bills which might come into
the possession of the Suffolk Bank; the latter bank
charging it interest whenever the amount redeemed
should exceed the funds to its credit; and if at any
time the excess should be greater than the permanent
deposit, the Suffolk Bank reserved the right of sending

(home the bills for specie redemption. As soon as the bills of any bank were charged to it, they were packed up as a special deposit, and held at the risk and subject to the order of the bank issuing them. In payment the Suffolk Bank received from any of the New England banks, with which it had opened an account, the bills of any New England bank in good standing *at par*, placing them to the credit of the bank sending them on the day following their receipt.

In 1831 redemption had increased so rapidly that the Suffolk Bank notified all its correspondents that thereafter it should charge them *daily* all their redeemed bills, keeping the same in special deposit, and subject to the order of the issuing bank. In the case, however, of the Rhode Island banks, whose bills were redeemed through the Merchants' Bank of Providence, the agreement was so far modified that the Suffolk Bank delivered all bills of that State in Providence at its own risk ; and the Merchants' Bank reciprocated, and delivered all the New England bills it sent to Boston for redemption to the Suffolk Bank, taking the same responsibility.) And now occurred the first robbery of the Suffolk Bank.

It had been the custom of the cashier, upon leaving the bank at the close of business, to enclose the bills of the Rhode Island banks, which were daily redeemed, in a leathern bag, which he deposited between the outer and the inner doors of the vault. The outer door of the vault was opened in the morning by Rand Lord, the porter, the bag taken out, and by him delivered to the driver of the Citizens' Coach Company, who carried it to Providence and delivered it to the Merchants' Bank of that city. On the morning of the twelfth of September, 1829, a man called at the bank quite early for the Providence bag, and the porter delivered it to him, although he was not one of the drivers of the Coach Company; still, as he had often seen him on the box with the driver, he suspected nothing wrong. Shortly after, the regular driver called for the bag; when it was discovered that the first man was a thief. This was the first loss of the kind the bank had sustained, and naturally there was great excitement. Messengers were sent in every direction, and a reward of one thousand dollars was offered for the recovery of the money, and one hundred dollars for the arrest of the robber. Within a month he was arrested, and all the money recovered except one hundred and fifteen dollars. This amount was charged to Rand Lord, to be taken out of his salary at the rate of ten dollars a month; the object being to make him more careful in the future, and for a warning to the other officers; as the transactions of the bank were of such a nature that the greatest care and vigilance were necessary at all times. In 1833 the amount was refunded to Lord. The expense of recovering the money, including the rewards paid, was $1,796.20, which was charged to profit and loss. The robber's name was John Wade.

Although the hostility to the Suffolk Bank had somewhat abated, as the system became more widely extended, and more and more country banks opened an account with it, still many of the weak ones felt that it was arbitrary and oppressive. The following letter written in 1832, by the cashier of the Suffolk Bank to the Bank of Rutland, Vermont, gives a good idea of the feeling then prevailing, and of the true position of the Suffolk Bank with regard to the New England banks ; as well as one of the principal reasons for requiring them to keep a permanent deposit. He writes : —

"We have never required you to redeem your bills at this bank instead of your own ; nor have we ever demanded of you 'an exorbitant price for counting your bills.' They will be received and counted at this bank whether you have a permanent deposit with us or not. We ask of you a permanent deposit as a consideration for receiving from you bills of all the other banks in the New England States in exchange for your own at par; some of which are converted into specie by us at a discount of one and a half per cent. In addition, we take the whole risk of those bills after they have been placed in our hands. We have now on hand $18,005, in bills of the Burrillville Bank, which has recently failed; whether we shall get pay for them or not is very doubtful. If you still think the price we ask for transacting your business is exorbitant, and should prefer paying your bills at your own counter, we have no objections to sending them there ; but we hope you will not expect us to take the bills of all the other banks in the New England States in payment for them at par. We have no intimation from other sources of a growing disaffection among the country banks ; and if we had, we should not feel ourselves obliged to transact their business without a reasonable compensation. On the contrary, gentlemen who were very much opposed to the system we have pursued, at its commencement, now express approbation of it, and their willingness to contribute to its support rather than it should be abandoned."

In July, 1831, the real estate, No. 60 State Street, now owned by the Suffolk National Bank, was purchased from the Massachusetts Mutual Fire Insurance Company for the sum of $57,000. The estate had a frontage of forty-three and three fourths feet on State Street, and an average depth of about one hundred and thirty-five feet. The buildings were old ; and in April of the following year the bank voted to improve the property, and appointed the President, with Messrs.

John Belknap and Jeffrey Richardson, a committee for that purpose. The front building was torn down, and the present granite and brick building erected in its place. The rear building was remodelled, and occupied by the foreign money department. The improvements were made at an expense of $51,895.11, to which was added a grant of one thousand dollars to Mr. Henry B. Stone, the President, for his extra services in attending to the same.

Between the years 1831 and 1833, a great increase took place in the number of banks in New England. During this period ninety new banks were chartered, of which forty-five were located in Massachusetts. The Suffolk Bank became overloaded with redeemed bills; the banks were slow in making remittances; and the accounts of many of them were overdrawn. Accordingly the Suffolk Bank sent a circular to such of its correspondents as it allowed to overdraw, informing them that on account of the scarcity of money, and in order to have some control over its own funds, overdrafts must be limited to ten thousand dollars. It also adopted the rule that foreign money deposits must be made before one o'clock, otherwise they would not be credited till the following business day. At the same time it reduced the permanent deposits required from the Boston banks to $15,000 as a minimum.

In September, 1833, the pressure in the money market became so great that it was found necessary to notify a large number of correspondents to make their accounts good; and that overdrafts would not be allowed. The following is a specimen of many letters written about this time : —

" DEAR SIR, — Your account is overdrawn about $16,000; and we shall send home your bills for specie on Monday next, if it is not made good on or before Saturday. We cannot permit any overdrafts on this bank in future, and shall hereafter send your bills home for payment unless you have funds here to redeem them as fast as received. We can allow no overdrafts, because banks are so numerous and money so scarce, that it has become necessary for each bank to rely entirely on its own resources, and to limit its business accordingly.

" Yours, very truly, etc., etc."

The directors at the same time passed a vote that " when notice is sent to any bank that its bills will be sent home for specie, unless its account is made good by a certain day, it shall be the duty of the President to carry it strictly into effect."

In 1834 the redemption business had increased five-fold, from $80,000 to $400,000 daily. The officers were employed till nearly midnight, and then often obliged to lay aside a large number of bills to be counted the next morning. To reduce the business, and keep it within bounds, it became necessary to modify the arrangement made with the Boston banks. Heretofore they had been allowed to send in *all* their foreign money at par, — now they could send in on any one day an amount equal to one half of their permanent deposit. If they exceeded that amount they were charged one tenth of one per cent. on the excess. They were also restricted to the foreign money received by them in the regular course of their business, excluding deposits from banks and brokers. By these means it was hoped the business could be brought within reasonable limits. At the same time the permanent deposit of the Boston banks was reduced to

$10,000; and in May, 1835, a further reduction was made to $5,000.

During the winter of 1835–36 thirty-two new banks were chartered in Massachusetts, making a total increase of seventy-eight new banks in this State during a period of six years, or more than double the number of banks in operation in 1830. And nearly the same ratio of increase took place in the number of banks in the New England States. In 1830 they numbered one hundred and sixty-nine; in 1837, three hundred and twenty-one. Many of these banks were started with little or no real capital; specie was borrowed for one day to be counted by the Bank Commissioner, and on the next it was replaced by the notes of the stockholders; the bills of these banks, loaned in violation of the usury laws at high rates of interest, were used in the wildest speculations. The country was flooded with them, and specie was becoming scarce. The ratio of specie to deposits and circulation had fallen to one to thirteen and a half, or less than seven and a half per cent., the smallest then ever known. These bills poured into the Suffolk Bank for redemption; and in April, 1836, it sent the following circular letter to forty-four banks, whose accounts were overdrawn in the aggregate sum of $664,000 : —

"Sir, — In consequence of the great increase of banks in the New England States during the past winter, and the scarcity of specie, it has become impracticable to allow any further overdrafts on this bank, or to hold your bills beyond the amount of funds to your credit. Your account is now overdrawn —— dollars, which we must rely upon your making good with as little delay as possible; and we shall be compelled to send your bills home for specie in future, unless you have funds here to redeem them. We regret the necessity of

4

these measures, but the deranged state of money matters throughout our whole country renders them unavoidable.

"Yours, etc.,   M. S. Parker, *Cashier.*"

Specie became scarcer every day, and the bank was constantly losing. On the twenty-fourth of June it paid Southern drafts in specie to the amount of $140,-000 ; besides which it furnished $50,000 to the Neponset Bank, which was to commence operations in a few days, and was under obligations to furnish $50,000 more to a new bank to be organized in Haverhill on the following Tuesday.

The pressure was so great that by November the Suffolk Bank had reduced its loan from $1,411,000 to $500,000, and was still suffering. So low had its specie reserve become, by reason of the overdrafts of the New England banks, that it was deemed advisable to put out no more of its own circulation ; discounts were at twenty-four per cent. per annum, and exchange was so high that the least advance would induce large shipments of specie to Europe. These were some of the indications of the coming storm which was to break upon the country the following year ; warnings of trouble which the managers of the bank were prompt to heed, and which they put the bank into a condition to meet.

The foreign money business was now so large, notwithstanding all the efforts to keep it within bounds, that it became necessary to increase Mr. Grubb's salary to $8,500 per annum, he assuming all loss by counterfeits and uncurrent or mutilated bills as heretofore. It was further agreed that he should turn over to the directors for destruction all bills of these descriptions which he had been obliged to make good, since he first took charge of the department. The amount was $1,475 only, an average of less than $150 a year, such great care and watchfulness had he exercised.

On the ninth of February, 1837, Mr. Matthew S. Parker resigned the office of cashier, having occupied the position nineteen years, and Mr. Isaac C. Brewer was elected in his place.

CHAPTER IV.

The threatening storm now broke. On the twelfth of May, 1837, the Suffolk Bank, in common with the other banks, suspended specie payments. The New York and Providence banks had suspended the day before, and the Boston banks must at once suspend, or lose all their specie. In such good condition had the bank been placed by its managers, that on the twenty-ninth of May the President wrote to Mr. Reuel Williams, of Augusta : —

"In regard to resuming specie payments, I can only say that we are ready to commence again to-day, and intend to remain in this condition till others are also ready. It will, however, be impossible for the banks generally to resume until we have a National Bank, or at least till exchange on England comes down to par."

The suspension of specie payments put an end at once to all coercive measures on the part of the Suffolk Bank, and consequently each bank was left to its own volition. Many of the banks continued to redeem their bills at the Suffolk as heretofore. The bills of these banks passed current all over the Union, and in some places even commanded a premium. Others withdrew their accounts, and the bills of these banks had a local circulation merely, and were current only in the immediate neighborhood of the bank issuing them. At first many of the weak banks, particularly the Maine banks, which had always been op-

posed to the Suffolk system, were inclined to break
off, and even some of the strong ones were in favor of
abandoning the system altogether. But sober second
thought led them to see the importance of sustaining
it, and they became convinced that it was for the
general good, as well as for their own interest; and
that, if the system were abandoned during the suspension of specie payments, the bank-note currency would
drift back into its old condition, when there were almost as many rates of discount as there were banks.

During this period a constant correspondence was
carried on, particularly with the Maine banks, many
of whose bills the Suffolk continued to receive, urging
them to continue in the system. In a communication
to the President of the Mercantile Bank, of Bangor,
occurs the following : —

"The Vermont banks have resolved to sustain the system, and the
Massachusetts, Connecticut, and New Hampshire banks, notwithstanding the inflammatory communications you have seen in the
papers, will do the same. We have been requested by several merchants, who are largely interested in the trade of Maine, to continue
to receive your bills, till they have had time to visit or communicate
with you on the subject."

Notwithstanding the efforts of the Suffolk Bank to
reduce the overdrafts of its correspondents, many of
them were unable to comply. This was more particularly the case with the Maine banks, many of
which were largely in its debt; and it was finally
obliged to decline to receive the bills of a large number of them. With these it made the best settlement
it could, in some instances taking a bond of indemnity
from the directors and prominent stockholders; in
others, real estate in Oldtown, Bangor, and other

places, most of which it was obliged to carry till 1842. Its total losses by Eastern banks were very great, and the confidence of the directors in the banks of this section of the New England States was very much impaired.

In April, 1838, the bank began to make preparations for resumption, and notified all its correspondents that they must make their accounts good on or before the first of July. Specie began to flow into the country from England, and resumption on bills of five dollars and under was at once commenced. Confidence was restored, — so much so that during the first week of resumption no bank in Boston was called upon for over five hundred dollars in specie on any one day, and in many banks more specie was deposited than was paid out.

Notice was sent to the Merchants' Bank of Providence, through which the bills of the Rhode Island banks were redeemed, that it must reduce its overdraft to $100,000. The Suffolk Bank, soon after suspension, had impressed upon the Rhode Island banks the importance of continuing the redemption system, and had offered them temporary aid to enable them to do so. This offer had been availed of by the Merchants' Bank, and its indebtedness now amounted to over $350,000, much to the inconvenience of the customers of the Suffolk Bank. In calling upon the Merchants' Bank to reduce this amount to $100,000, Mr. Stone, the President, writes : " I hope you will take measures to induce the banks of your State to reduce their circulation to their means of redeeming as early as possible." This the Rhode Island banks were slow to do; and in July, and again in September, Mr. Stone in-

formed the Merchants' Bank that the Suffolk was suffering great inconvenience by the overdrafts of the
Rhode Island banks, and unless the amount was speed-
ily reduced he should send home their bills for specie,
of which he was much in need, as the Suffolk was then
redeeming for over three hundred banks; money was
very scarce, and he had been unable for some weeks
to make any discounts. In December a new arrangement was made with the Merchants' Bank, and the
amount of overdraft was fixed at $50,000, with the
understanding that, if the banks of that State could
not keep themselves in a condition to meet this limit,
the Suffolk would decline to receive their bills.

Early this year the Suffolk drew its balance from the
United States Bank, and received in payment United
States Bank notes, guaranteed to be paid in specie
upon resumption. These notes the directors of the
Suffolk authorized their cashier to indorse to the
amount of $200,000. It also authorized him to issue
them; to receive them on deposit; and to pay them
in specie upon resumption.

The Suffolk Bank had now a monopoly of the foreign
money business; it had paid to its stockholders an
annual average dividend of eight and eight-tenths per
cent. during the past five years; and in September,
1839, it was voted to increase the capital to one million dollars. At the same time an extra dividend of
thirty-three and one third per cent. was declared out
of its surplus profits; which enabled the stockholders
to take one new share for each three old shares held
by them, and pay for the same with the extra dividend.
In addition, a dividend of three per cent. was paid
the following month on the increased capital. Not-

withstanding the prosperity of the bank, the directors
at all times held its officers to the strictest accountabil-
ity. In October of this year an examination of the
bank showed a loss of $1,040, arising from Windsor
Bank notes, which the clerks in the foreign money
department had taken after they had been ordered to
throw them out. This amount was charged to Mr.
Grubb, in accordance with the terms of the agreement
made with him; and the cashier was ordered to with-
hold two hundred dollars per month from his salary till
the amount was paid.

In 1841 the United States issued a loan of twelve
million dollars, with interest at the rate of five and two
fifths per cent., payable quarterly. Of this amount the
Suffolk Bank took $500,000. During the year, how-
ever, money became very scarce, and the directors
adopted the policy of discounting only the shortest
paper, fixing their extreme limit to three months. In
a letter to the President of the Bangor Bank, who had
applied for a discount to enable him to make the
account of that bank good, the President of the Suffolk, under date of the twenty-fifth October, says : —

"Our discount sheet has been entirely closed for some time past;
and our board will not consent to discount for any one. If the water
ran in the Penobscot as freely as the specie has run from our vaults
since the first instant, you would have no difficulty in getting your
lumber to market. I am glad you are so situated as to hear the
thunder before the lightning reaches you."

By the first of December money had become so
scarce, and the pressure so great, that notice was sent
to one hundred and three banks, whose accounts were
overdrawn, that unless they at once made their accounts good their bills would be sent home for specie;

and a vote was passed to honor the draft of no bank
beyond the funds to the credit of the drawer. On the
twenty-fifth of the month, Massachusetts bonds, payable
in 1858, sold at eighty-six, the lowest price then ever
known.

On the seventh of March, 1842, Mr. Samuel Hubbard
resigned the position of director, to take a seat upon
the Supreme Bench of Massachusetts. Mr. Hubbard
had served the bank from the beginning, twenty-four
years, and during that time had been its legal adviser.
The following correspondence shows the esteem in
which he was held by his brother directors : —

" To THE PRESIDENT AND DIRECTORS OF THE SUFFOLK BANK.

" GENTLEMEN, — In consequence of having accepted the appoint-
ment to a seat on the bench of the Supreme Judicial Court of the
Commonwealth, it will be inconvenient for me to continue longer in
the direction of the Suffolk Bank. Having been a member of the
board from the institution of the bank to the present time, I cannot
retire from it without expressing my approbation of the manner in
which its important and complicated business is managed, and my
kind feelings towards all the members of the board.

" Wishing you all prosperity, I am, gentlemen, very respectfully,
" Your friend and servant,
" SAMUEL HUBBARD."

" BOSTON, *March* 28, 1842.

" DEAR SIR, — Your letter of the 7th inst., addressed to the President and Directors of the Suffolk Bank, has been referred to us with
instructions to reciprocate on their behalf in the fullest manner the
feelings of personal regard which you are kind enough to express
towards them individually.

" For the wisdom of the counsels and the heartiness of coöperation
with which you have aided them during a long course of service as a
director; and especially for the firmness and assiduity with which at
a critical period you managed the business of the institution as President, they beg leave to tender you their sincere acknowledgments.

" They still indulge the hope that you will not find it incompatible with the duties of the high office to which you have been called to allow your name to remain in the direction of the bank. As a stockholder you would not sit in any case where its interests were involved; and any advice you might give in important matters (and to such we will limit our requisitions), could not prejudice your judicial action.

      " We are with great respect,

          " Very truly yours,

              WILLIAM LAWRENCE, } *Committee.*
              J. A. LOWELL.

" HON. SAMUEL HUBBARD,

       " *Judge Supreme Court.*"

CHAPTER V.

Circulation based upon specie, and loans upon strictly mercantile paper, were two of the cardinal principles in the directors' system of banking. This is well illustrated in a letter written in 1842 to Job Lyman, President of the Bank of Woodstock : —

"It appears evident from your letter of the 16th inst. that too large a portion of your loan is in accommodation paper, which cannot be relied upon at maturity to meet your liabilities; and that your chief reliance, or means for reducing your balance or debt at this bank, is upon an expansion of your circulation, which you probably expect will arise from the 'coming clip of wool in your State,' and from the 'wisdom of our country assembled at Washington.' The former no doubt may afford you some relief, and we hope you may be aided by the latter : but the experience of the last twelve years strongly indicates that it is not so safe a basis for circulation as gold or silver or good mercantile paper. Since you are now placed at the head of the institution we hope you will take measures to change the character of your loan, and render it more available in case of need.

"Your account is now overdrawn about $18,000, and if the other New England banks were as much in arrears as you, it would require a capital of five and a half millions to supply their wants. If the United States loan should be taken up by the capitalists of New England, or exchange on England should advance one half of one per cent., it would bring a severe pressure upon our money market and oblige us to call for our balances. We hope, therefore, you will take measures to reduce your balance immediately. Our discount sheet is entirely closed, and we do not even look at the applications."

Strict justice and impartiality also governed the directors in their action towards banks keeping an account with them. It was always their aim to treat all their correspondents alike, and to make no concessions to one that they did not make to all others. Constant applications were made for an allowance of interest on the permanent deposits. These were invariably denied on the ground that no preferences could be given.

In all the agreements made with country banks it was inserted that they should make all collections in their towns for the Suffolk Bank free of charge, which should be charged to them seven days after maturity; the Suffolk Bank on its part agreeing to make all their collections in Boston at par, and those elsewhere at the regular rates of exchange. The country banks, forgetting their agreement, and laboring under the impression that the Suffolk Bank was making too much profit out of them, would often charge a half of one per cent. for making collections. This invariably led to a remonstrance on the part of the Suffolk, and sharp correspondence often ensued.

In June, 1842, the Bank of Montpelier made such a charge, and justified itself on the ground that the charge was made, not for collecting, but for remitting the proceeds to Boston. The President of the Suffolk Bank says in reply : " And what is the character of these proceeds? Not specie or its equivalent, but chiefly the bills of upwards of three hundred banks, some of which we are obliged to send as far as from here to Montpelier to collect, and at an expense of more than one per cent." ; — and then in reply to certain remarks indicating that the old feeling against the Suffolk system had not died out : —

" Your remarks in relation to the Associated Banks indicate that you are under a misapprehension, as no such association has been in existence for carrying on the foreign money business for more than eighteen years. The Suffolk Bank stands upon its own responsibility, independent and free as the Bank of Montpelier; and we feel competent to judge of what is just and proper in our arrangements with other banks. If we have been successful in our business it has not been owing to the banks in your State. The loss we sustained by the Windsor Bank alone was nearly equal to the amount of permanent deposits we ever received from all the other banks."

Undoubted security was likewise a paramount principle controlling the directors; and so United States treasury notes and Massachusetts bonds were favorite investments. On the first day of April, 1844, the loan of the bank amounted to $3,026,714; of which amount $948,800 was in these securities; and a large part of the balance was in demand loans to the New England banks, being overdrafts bearing interest, for which the bank held their circulating notes, payable on demand in specie, as collateral. And herein lay the great power of the Suffolk Bank. A pressure upon it from any cause induced it at once to notify the debtor banks to pay their overdrafts, on penalty of having their bills sent home for specie. The country banks kept their circulation as extended as possible for their own profit. Their overdrafts on the Suffolk enabled them to do so; but at the same time it put them completely into its power. The weaker and the more extended they were by reason of their ignorance of the principles of sound banking, or their desire for large profits, the more difficult they found it to respond, till the time came when the Suffolk discredited their bills. Then they found themselves in a very uncomfortable position; and realized the truth of Poor Richard's maxim, "The borrower is slave of the lender."

It must not be inferred that the Suffolk Bank encouraged any such expansion of their circulation; on the contrary, the Suffolk Bank system was established for contracting it, and all its efforts were exerted in that direction. And although the overdrafts were a source of profit, still its constant effort was to keep them within reasonable and safe limits, and so keep their circulation in the same bounds. In a letter to the Eastern Bank of Bangor, the President of the Suffolk says: —

" Your proposal has been laid before our board again to-day ; but our directors decline discounting any more paper for you at present. They were in hopes that the discount of $18,000 a few days since would enable your bank to keep its account good ; but it has been behind-hand again about $23,000, which they wish you to cover in ; at any rate they will not consent to its being increased. With the new tariff and sub-treasury staring in our faces we think it unwise for the banks to expand. I can only say if all the banks in New England were moving on at the same rate you are, it would require more than all the capital of the banks in this city to supply their wants."

Constant warnings like the above run through all the correspondence of the bank. Neither was the bank willing to enter into correspondence with any new banks for the redemption of their bills, thus giving them credit, unless it was satisfied the public would be safe in taking them, although itself might be reasonably secure. as in all cases it required a permanent deposit for the redemption of bills, and kept the matter of overdrafts entirely in its own hands. Overtures for the opening of such accounts were sometimes received, but invariably rejected.

About this time an arrangement was made with bankers and others in New York State to receive from them New England bills at one tenth of one per cent. discount.

In 1846, Mr. Grubb's salary was raised to $10.800, on the same terms as heretofore; and he handed over to the foreign money committee, for destruction, all the counterfeit, mutilated and failed bills, etc., which had been charged to his account since 1836; the total amount was $2,442, as per the following schedule: —

Counterfeits	$1107 00
Broken banks . .	766 00
Alterations .	221 00
Specimens . . .	89 00
Counterfeit signatures	72 00
Globe Bank, Bangor .	120 00
Fulton Bank, Boston	67 00

In 1847 redemptions had increased to such an extent that it became almost impossible to count the foreign money received daily; and large amounts had to be laid aside for the next day; thus increasing the next day's labor, which frequently had to be thrown on to the third day. The directors felt it exceedingly important that each day should accomplish its own work. Accordingly they increased Mr. Grubb's salary to $14,000 per annum; and two years later they raised it to $20,000; at which time he handed over to them for destruction the counterfeit and uncurrent bills redeemed by him since 1846, amounting to $2,020.

About this time a discrepancy was discovered in the accounts of the receiving teller. His book-keeping was very careless; and an examination of his books showed many omissions, and frequent double credits; besides which his balances were forced. The total deficiency amounted to $2,932.92. He was dismissed, and his bondsmen notified to make the loss good. A settlement was effected with them for $1,000, and the difference was charged to profit and loss. Early the next year a letter was received enclosing thirty-eight dollars, "overpayment to a country bank some twenty years ago," signed "Conscience." This money was given to Mr. Grubb, as it evidently belonged to the foreign money department. How much the late receiving teller's conscience troubled him the directors never knew; nor could they ever fully decide whether he was a knave, or whether his losses were the result of carelessness. He would have had the credit of the latter opinion, had he not finally forced his balances. This gave a dark look to his transactions.

On the fifteenth of June, 1849, Mr. Henry B. Stone died, having served as President twenty-three years, and to him, *under the careful guidance and wise counsel of the foreign money committee,* was due the great measure of success which the bank had attained. His labors were constant and persevering, and the system had now so gained the support of all the sound and conservative banks of New England, that, had the Suffolk given up the redemption of foreign money, a new agency for carrying on the work would have been established. On the twenty-ninth of the same month Mr. Jeffrey Richardson was elected President. He had been a director since 1823, and had served on the foreign money committee constantly since its establishment in 1825. The business of the bank continued to increase so fast, that in October more space was required in which to conduct its operations. Accordingly application was made to the Atlas Bank, occupying rooms on the second floor of the bank building, to dispose of its lease, for which a bonus of one thousand dollars was demanded and paid. At the same time notice was given that no bills for redemption would be received unless they were assorted into two packages, one containing Boston bills only, and the other the issues of other banks. At first some of the banks resisted, but the firm determination of the Suffolk to receive them in no other way resulted in an acquiescence on their part, without which it would have been almost impossible to accomplish the daily work. Notice was also given that no more redemptions would be made for individuals, private bankers, or brokers.

On the fifth of October, 1850, occurred the second robbery of the bank. On this occasion a bag of gold containing five thousand dollars had been brought in from a neighboring bank in settlement of a balance, and placed by the messenger on the counter of the teller; his attention was called off for a moment, when a man, who had probably followed the messenger for the purpose, seized the bag and ran. He was at once followed, but evaded the pursuit. The money was never recovered, and the amount was charged to profit and loss.

The average daily redemptions were now about seven hundred and fifty thousand dollars, and the business was very remunerative. Since the extra dividend of thirty-three and a third per cent. in 1839, the bank had paid dividends to its stockholders of eight per cent. annually to 1847, and from 1847 to 1852 ten per cent. annually, besides which it had accumulated a surplus of $330,000.

But this surplus was not to be divided among the stockholders, as in 1839. On the twenty-third of March, 1852, the book-keeper of the bank informed the officers that he had received a telegram from New York, advising him that his brother was sick in that

6

city, and requesting him to come on at once. Permission was given, and he left his post. On the morning of the twenty-fourth the receiving teller did not make his appearance, and during the day a message was received from the New York police, informing the bank that they had arrested the latter on board a steamer about sailing for Europe, that the book-keeper was supposed to be on board the same steamer, and asking what should be done with them. This was the first intimation the bank had that anything was wrong. Instructions were at once sent to hold them; and an investigation of the affairs of the bank was begun, when it was discovered that there was a deficiency of $214,518.13. Upon the person of the teller was found $5,100 in gold, which was restored to the bank. He was brought to Boston for trial, and, pleading guilty, received for sentence one day solitary confinement and three years hard labor in the State's prison. This sentence was not fully served out. At the expiration of a year and a half he obtained a pardon, through the influence of his friends. He gave up $2,661.09 belonging to the bank, and one Rutland Railroad bond of the value of $1,014.12, besides which a check for $913.02 was returned to the bank which was said to belong to him. The book-keeper escaped to Callao, where he died, troubled in conscience for his wrong-doing.

The net loss to the bank by the rascality of these two officers was $205,780.24, which was charged to the surplus account. It turned out that they had been extensive speculators in stocks. At one time they had made more than $100,000 in Reading Railroad stock, but had afterwards lost it in a corner in the stock of the Canton Company. In October of the previous

year, just after the semi-annual examination of the
bank by the directors, they began to sell stocks short
very heavily in New York through a broker in that
city; the market suddenly rose, and they were tempted
to take money and send it to New York to make their
margins good. The whole amount was stolen between
the two semi-annual examinations; they knew it was
about time for the April examination; that then the
defalcation must be discovered; and they sought safety
in flight.

At the time of the teller's arrest by the officers in
New York they were as ignorant of the defalcation in
the Suffolk Bank as were the officers of that institution themselves. Some years previous he had been
employed in the Thames Bank at Norwich, in which
his brother-in-law was also employed. These two
young men had been in the habit of bringing to Boston the money from the Norwich banks for redemption; taking the night express to Boston and return-
ing the next day, carrying back the currency of the
Norwich banks that had been redeemed by the Suffolk
Bank. One night while on the way to take the train
at Norwich, between the bank and the station the
brother-in-law of the teller was knocked down, very
badly wounded, and robbed of his valise containing
the money for redemption. Detectives were at once
put upon the track both in New York and Boston.
But no clue to the money or the robber was ever
found. Some time after he came to Boston, and found
employment as teller in the Suffolk Bank. From that
time he was "shadowed" by the Norwich detectives, although the fact was unknown to the officers of that
bank; nor had they ever known that any suspicion

had attached to him. The afternoon he left Boston to
go to New York it was known to the detectives; and
they, suspecting something wrong, hastened to New
York, and caused his arrest on board the steamer the
next morning. They supposed they had recovered
part of the money stolen from the Norwich Bank; and
it was not until after the steamer had sailed that they
discovered that the money found upon the teller did
not belong to the Norwich Bank, but "to the old con-
cern in Boston," as he expressed it. The book-keeper
was on board at the time, but seeing the arrest of his
accomplice made his escape before he was discovered
by the officers.

So great a defalcation would have been impossible
by a single officer; but by the connivance of two the
affair was concealed for a long time; although it must
necessarily have been discovered at the next semi-annual examination of the bank by the directors. Notwithstanding the magnitude of the loss, the business of
the bank was so prosperous that the directors felt justified in paying in April the usual semi-annual dividend of five per cent.

During the summer of this year, the bank at South
Royalston, Vt., desired to make an arrangement with
the Suffolk differing from that usually made with other
banks. This the Suffolk, in justice to its other correspondents, declined to do, and notified the South Royalston Bank that, unless the usual terms were complied
with, it should send home for specie a large amount of
bills then on hand. Accordingly a messenger was sent
with $10,000 in bills of that bank, with orders to de-
mand payment in specie. Instead of paying, by some
process of Vermont law the bills were attached and

the messenger put under arrest. A novel way of paying one's promises! A writ of replevin was at once taken out, and the attachment dissolved. At the same time notice was given that no more bills of the South Royalston Bank would be received by the Suffolk. At the request of the other banks in Vermont the difficulty was finally adjusted, the South Royalston Bank acceding to the usual terms.

In 1853 it was found necessary again to increase the appropriation for the foreign money department. Mr. Grubb's salary was raised to $24,000 per annum, and a gratuity of $1,700 was divided among the officers of the banking department for their assistance in the foreign money department during the past year.

CHAPTER VI.

THE banks of New England were divided into two classes : those keeping a deposit with the Suffolk Bank and redeeming their bills at its counter; and those which kept an account with some other Boston bank, with which an arrangement was made for the redemption of their bills. The Suffolk Bank did not require the New England banks to keep a deposit with it as a condition precedent to receiving their bills at par. On the contrary, it received at par the bills of all sound New England banks, whether they kept an account with it or not. It only required that they should redeem their bills at some convenient place on penalty of having them sent home for specie.

For the bills of the former class of banks the Suffolk had security in the form of deposits and collections. For the bills of the other class it had no security except the good faith of the banks acting as their agents, and to which it charged and sent daily all the bills for the redemption of which they were responsible. As these could not be sent till the day after they were received, the Suffolk Bank was actually taking the risk of redemption on all this class of bills for one day without any security; and should any of these banks fail it had no positive assurance that the redeeming bank, with which such failed bank kept an account, would receivefromu it the bills it might have in hand.

Early in 1853 the Eastern Bank of West Killingly and the Woodbury Bank of Connecticut got into trouble, and the Boston bank with which they kept their accounts, and which acted as their agent, declined to receive from the Suffolk the bills of these two banks which it had on hand. The directors at once instructed the cashier to send the following circular to those banks in Boston which acted as agents in redeeming the bills of country banks: —

"Suffolk Bank, Boston, *March* 21, 1853.

"To the President and Directors of the ———— Bank.

"Gentlemen, — In receiving at par the bills of New England banks we have not required that they should keep their accounts with us, but have given them the option of keeping them in other banks in Boston. It is obvious, however, that in such cases we must rely for our security upon the assurance, expressed or implied, that those Boston banks which act as agents in paying the bills of other banks would continue to redeem the bills taken by us in our regular business until after notice to the contrary. Without such assurance, the collections and deposits, in other words, all the security, would be in the hands of one party, while all the risk was incurred by the other.

"We cannot believe that any other interpretation of the existing arrangements could be seriously contemplated; but to preclude any possible doubt, we take the liberty of stating in terms, that we receive the bills of all those country banks, that are sent into other Boston banks for redemption, for account and at the risk of such Boston banks until after notice shall be given to us of their intention to discontinue such redemption.

"If you have any bank accounts that you cannot continue on these terms, please advise us of such bank, that we may either discontinue receiving their bills, or notify them that a different arrangement must be made. Respectfully yours,

"I. C. Brewer, *Cashier.*"

To this circular very few of the banks made any reply. By their silence they accepted it as a notice from the Suffolk Bank, by the terms of which they were to be bound in future transactions. The Exchange Bank of Boston sent a protest declining to be bound by its requirements. This bank had the accounts of some twenty country banks, and was acting as their agent. Unless the Exchange Bank complied with the terms of the circular the Suffolk must throw out the bills of all these banks. Before doing so, however, it sent a letter to each of the country banks, correspondents of the Exchange, making a plain statement of the facts. The country banks were naturally very much displeased at the action of the Exchange Bank. They regarded it as a want of confidence in their credit, and ten or more of them at once transferred their accounts to the Suffolk.

About this time an effort was being made to establish a bank in opposition to the Suffolk. As yet it had met with no favor from the Boston banks. Its principal supporters had been out of town banks, who for one reason or another had become prejudiced against the Suffolk. But now the enterprise was joined by the Exchange Bank, which felt itself aggrieved at the action of the Suffolk, and all its influence was exerted to carry the project to a successful termination. This was not accomplished till some years later. But there is little doubt that the circular the twenty-first of March was one of the remote causes which led to the establishment of the Bank of Mutual Redemption.

The country banks opposed to the Suffolk naturally exerted their powers to annoy it, and sometimes they were very ingenious. One of the most strenuous opponents of the Suffolk Bank system was the Veazie Bank of Bangor. Through its instrumentality a law was passed in Maine giving the banks of that State a certain delay, after demand at their counters, in which to redeem their bills in specie. The Veazie Bank availed itself of the time allowed, which it used to the annoyance of the Suffolk Bank. Having received in the regular course of its business a quantity of Veazie Bank notes, the Suffolk Bank would send a messenger to Bangor and demand specie for the same. The bank would acknowledge the demand and claim the lawful delay. In the mean time it would collect Boston funds and send them to a well-known Boston broker, who, himself no friend of the Suffolk Bank, would take great pleasure in exchanging them in one way and another for checks on that bank. He would then present himself at the bank, demand specie for his checks, and with the coin thus obtained pay it for the bills for which it had demanded specie some days before : in short, not only requiring the Suffolk Bank to hold the bills of the Veazie Bank for a certain specified time, but at the end of that time to furnish specie for their redemption.

On the twenty-fifth of July, 1853, the cashier, Mr. I. C. Brewer, tendered his resignation, having served the bank in this capacity sixteen years, and having been in its employ thirty years. His resignation was accepted, his salary continued to the end of the year, and he was invited to visit the bank from time to time, as his convenience might enable him, and render such assistance to the new cashier as he might find agreeable. On the sixth of August, Mr. Edward Tyler was elected in his stead, and on the first of September he entered upon the duties of the office.

The receipts of foreign money were now so large

that it was impossible to finish the daily counting and assorting till nearly midnight. To expedite matters, a circular was sent to the Boston banks to the effect that no New England money would be received from them later than twelve o'clock each day. This was found necessary because many of the Boston banks did not make their deposits till nearly three o'clock, and the redemptions on some days amounted to almost a million dollars. The banks demurred, and a modification was made whereby they were allowed till one o'clock to send in their foreign money; and that which they received between one and two o'clock they sent in to the Suffolk the next morning; for this it gave them Suffolk funds payable that day.

During this year it was deemed expedient to make extensive alterations in the interior of the bank building for the use of the foreign money department, and the matter was put in charge of the President. At the annual meeting in October, Mr. Richardson accepted a reëlection with much reluctance, as his health was not good, and he felt that he should necessarily be absent from his duties much of the time. The directors, however, prevailed upon him to continue in office, and appointed Mr. William W. Tucker to attend to the affairs of the bank during his absence.

In April, 1854, his health still failing him, Mr. Richardson sent in his resignation, and Mr. J. Amory Davis was elected in his stead. Upon accepting the resignation a vote was passed recognizing the high sense entertained by the directors of the value of Mr. Richardson's long, faithful, and efficient services as President and director; and, at the same time, a committee was appointed to make some suitable acknowledgment to

Mr. Richardson for his extra labor in superintending the alterations in the building for the use of the foreign money department, to which he had given much attention. This same committee was also charged with the duty of making a like recognition of the value of Mr. Tucker's services in attending to the duties of the President during his absence on account of sickness. In accordance with these votes a silver vase was presented to Mr. Tucker, and three pieces of plate — pitcher, vase, and salver — to Mr. Richardson.

Soon after the election of the new President, Mr. Grubb laid before the directors a statement of the expenses of the foreign money department, showing them to have been $31,600 for the year, including his deficit at the time his salary was raised to $24,000. Accordingly, it was voted to pay Mr. Grubb $7,600 to make up to him the deficit to date, and to fix the salary for the present at $27,000 per annum. Six months later the business had increased to so great an extent that it became necessary to appropriate $30,000 for the annual expenses of the department, and to make preparation for the enlargement of the premises occupied by it.

The sum of $8,000 was collected this year from the bondsmen of the late defaulting teller, in addition to which he himself returned $1,200.

In December, 1854, Mr. Grubb informed the directors that the losses in his department from the fifth of October, 1853, to the second of August, 1854, had amounted to $11,098, in addition to which there were unsettled claims of various banks aggregating $2,200. This department now employed seventy clerks; and the accommodations were such that the counting and assorting could not be carried on in one room, under the eye of a single overseer. The directors at once took the matter in hand, and instituted a private examination of each member of the department. They also made a careful inquiry into every suspicious circumstance that had come to their knowledge, but they failed to fix any guilt upon any employé. They found the character of most of the clerks to be unexceptionable. Six, however, whose habits were calculated to invite suspicion, were discharged; but even in these cases there was no actual evidence of dishonesty.

In December, 1855, the difficulties attending the business had become so great that the propriety of giving up the whole system or of dividing the business between two banks was seriously discussed. After much earnest consideration of the matter it was finally decided to continue as before, and for that purpose to enlarge the building. Accordingly, a committee was appointed to petition the Legislature for leave to increase the investment in real estate. The petition was granted by the Senate, but rejected by the House. To obtain enlarged accommodations the rear land was leased to the National Insurance Company, who erected a building thereon and leased the same to the bank for a term of ten years; at the expiration of which time, the lease to the insurance company expiring, the buildings would belong to the bank. At the same time the building on State Street was improved and made fireproof at an expense of $38,493.68, which was charged to profit and loss.

In order to give the clerks in the foreign money department a pecuniary interest in securing the utmost accuracy and fidelity in its business, a fund was created for their benefit. To this fund five thousand dollars was to be credited annually, and to it were to be charged the losses in the department, and the interest of the balance was to be divided among the clerks. But the losses more than counterbalanced the fund, and nothing was gained to them. Premiums for accuracy were also tried, but the losses still continued. In October, 1855, $14,211.27 was paid on this account, and in October, 1856, $7,728.06. That these losses were not always attributable to dishonesty is evidenced by the fact that on one occasion, shortly after there had been a loss in this department of $2,929, the President received through the post-office an envelope inclosing the same amount, with a memorandum attached, " Lost by carelessness."

In July, 1857, $40,000 was appropriated for the expenses of the foreign money department. This was the largest amount that was ever appropriated for the business. The redemptions for the year amounted to $400,000,000. This amount, for New England alone, is nearly double the amount redeemed for the whole United States for the fiscal year 1876–77, by the Redemption Bureau at Washington, under the United States Bank Act. This department, during that year, redeemed $214,361,300 at an expense of $167,704.05, as follows : —

For salaries . . .	. $150,695 68
Printing and binding	6,604 30
Stationery . . .	3,818 10
Postage . . .	3,716 66
Contingent expenses . .	. 2,869 31
	$167,704 05

showing the cost of assorting and counting the bills by the United States to have been over seventy cents per $1,000 for salaries alone, while the Suffolk Bank assorted and counted $400,000,000 in 1857 at an expense for salaries of $40,000, or ten cents per $1,000; the United States Redemption Bureau thus expending seven times as much as did the Suffolk Bank to do the same work. It is true that the United States Bureau assorts and counts the bills of two thousand banks; while the Suffolk assorted and counted the bills of five hundred banks only. But this is counterbalanced by the fact that all the national banks are numbered and the notes of each bear across their face a number in red ink twice imprinted, indicating the number of the bank, so that they can be readily and easily assorted by numbers; while the Suffolk Bank was obliged to assort by names, a much more difficult and tedious task. The national bank notes are moreover printed from similar plates and on the same quality of paper, all furnished by the Comptroller of the Currency, making it easy to detect counterfeits and altered bills; while the notes which the Suffolk Bank counted and assorted were printed from almost as many plates, and on as various qualities of paper, as there were banks.

The expense of the Redemption Bureau at Washington has to be borne by the national banks, in addition to keeping with the Treasurer at Washington a permanent deposit equal to five per cent. of the entire circulation of the banks, a greater permanent deposit proportionately than was required by the Suffolk Bank, for the use alone of which it was contented to bear all the expense, and take all the risk of redemption; a risk which, so far as the United States Treasurer is

concerned, is nothing, as he has collateral security in
his hands for all redemptions in the form of United
States bonds at ninety cents on the dollar.

/ If the local banks of New England had any just
cause of complaint against the Suffolk Bank and its
system, well might the national banks of to-day protest against the expenses of the Redemption Bureau.
That no such protest is made may be attributed to the
useful lessons taught by the Suffolk Bank, namely,
that the bank currency of a country, to be sound and
healthy, must be redeemable at some central point;
that the more certain the community is of its redemption upon demand the more widely it will circulate,
thus benefiting both the banks and the public; and
that consequently the banks should complain of no
reasonable expense that will accomplish so desirable
an object. The history of the Suffolk Bank amply
proves that such a purpose might be effected by private enterprise at less expense, and yet with as much
safety to the public.

During the five years preceding 1857 a large increase of banks took place in New England. In 1852
the number was three hundred and sixty-one, and in
1857, five hundred and four. Speculation was ram-
pant, merchandise of all kinds had advanced in price,
and the bank loans were very high, while the specie
reserve was low, being less than nine per cent. of the
circulation and deposits. The loans had increased
from $147,839,000 in 1852 to $192,450,000 in 1857;
so that the banks were in a very poor condition to
withstand the panic which then took place. The
directors of the Suffolk Bank had prepared themselves to meet the coming crisis, and had reduced their

loans from $2,009,646.69 on the first day of April, to $1,409,641.74 on the first day of October. On the third of the month they voted to hold daily meetings, and on the fourteenth, in common with the other banks, and in accordance with the recommendation of the clearing house, they voted to suspend specie payments, recording the following vote : —

"That specie payments be suspended by this bank for a season; but that the business be conducted with reference to a resumption at the earliest practicable time; and that in the opinion of this board specie payments might and would have been continued in Boston but for the unfortunate action in New York."

In common with the other banks the Suffolk resumed the following year.

Early in October, before the suspension, when the pressure on the banks was very great, a committee from the banks of Springfield, Massachusetts, fearing that the Suffolk would throw out the bills of some of the banks in the western part of the State, waited upon Mr. J. Amory Davis, the President, asking the Suffolk Bank to sustain the banks in Springfield. The matter was referred to the directors, who voted that the President reply to the committee that —

"At the present time there is no intention to strike off any particular bank in Springfield, or elsewhere in the western part of the State; but that it is impossible for the Suffolk Bank, in justice to itself, or the country or city banks of New England, to pledge itself to sustain any one bank or class of banks; that it must judge in each particular case as it may arise what it may be its duty to do; and further, that it is disposed to continue the same liberality in general to the country banks which the committee has so handsomely acknowledged has been its practice heretofore."

CHAPTER VII.

THERE had now for some years been a growing impression that the redemption of foreign money was very profitable to the Suffolk Bank ; and the country banks felt that an agency might be established in Boston, in the profits of which, as stockholders, they might share. There was also the old feeling of ill-will among the weak banks, which had been compelled to keep their circulation within bounds. These were glad to join any enterprise which, while offering the prospect of more liberal terms and at the same time of profit, would do anything towards checking the prosperity of the Suffolk, and breaking up what they considered an unjust monopoly.

Accordingly, an application was made to the Legislature, and in 1855 a charter was granted to the Bank of Mutual Redemption. This bank did not go into operation till 1858; and then, so firmly grounded in the good opinion of the Boston banks was the Suffolk system, it met with great opposition, not only from the Suffolk Bank, but also from the other banks connected with the clearing house, which denied it admission to that association.

Many of the country banks interested in the Mutual Redemption at once withdrew their permanent deposits from the Suffolk, and requested it to send any

8

bills of their issue which might come into its possession to the new bank for redemption. This the Suffolk declined to do, because the new bank kept no
permanent deposit with it; and consequently it could
not receive current money from it in exchange without giving it an advantage over the Boston banks,
which paid for the privilege by a deposit; thus doing
for the Mutual Redemption gratuitously what all the
other banks paid it for doing, and so virtually breaking up the system.

Much confusion was naturally the result, and between the two stools some of the country banks feared
they might come to the ground. Having withdrawn
their permanent deposit from the Suffolk, and that
bank declining to send their bills for redemption to the
new bank, they were anxious lest it should send them
home and demand specie. Not keeping an account
with the new bank, and the Suffolk declining to receive
current money from it, they were fearful that the
Bank of Mutual Redemption would send their bills
home for the same purpose.

Finally, after much correspondence between the two
banks, an understanding was arrived at on the ninth of
March, 1859; each bank agreeing to receive from the
other such bills as either might receive in the regular
course of the business of banks keeping an account
with it. This arrangement was continued till the
twenty-second of March, 1860, when it was broken
off on account of a disagreement as to when the responsibility on the redeemed bills of the Rhode Island
banks should cease.

In the mean time, about one half of the banks in
New England had transferred their accounts to the

Bank of Mutual Redemption; and on the first of November, 1858, the Suffolk discontinued the regular business of counting and assorting country money. It signified, however, its willingness to receive such money at the rate of twenty-five cents per thousand dollars; and many of the Boston banks made an arrangement with it on this basis. It also continued to receive from country banks, which kept a satisfactory account with it, such country money as they might have occasion to send it in the way of remittance. This business it continued till 1866, and elected annually a foreign money committee to take charge of it.

In giving up the business the directors made the following record : —

"The Suffolk Bank has had for many years no motive beyond that of securing to the community a continuance of the acknowledged benefits of the system. The labor, expense, and risks of the business have been equal to any remuneration received from the use of the deposits. We cannot consent any longer to have the bank placed in the position, as is charged against us, of carrying on the business merely for its profits ; nor can we be expected to stand out against public opinion, prejudiced and excited, in sustaining a system, however beneficial to the public, after it has become unremunerative and hazardous to the stockholders of the bank. If public sentiment is now against it, and if it is less appreciated by the trading community and the city banks than heretofore, the cause is not to be found in the mode of pursuing it. The time has arrived for surrendering our agency in the system as heretofore conducted. Our responsibility in it must cease, because its main feature, the right to send home bills for specie, cannot be given up without destroying its efficacy ; because our exercise of this right is effectually made use of by those hostile to the Suffolk Bank system to place the bank in a false attitude before the public ; and because, under existing circumstances, the bank does not wish to stand in the way of a trial of the attempted experiment of a foreign money system to be conducted on less stringent principles."

It was the underlying principle of the Suffolk Bank system that any bank issuing circulation should keep itself at all times in a condition to be able to redeem it; that it should measure the amount by its ability so to do; and that the exercise at any time of the right to demand specie of a bank for its bills was something of which the issuing bank had no right to complain. The directors enunciated this principle when they first entered into the foreign money business, in their controversy with the agent of the Springfield Bank in 1824; they acted upon it during the whole existence of the system, and they gave up the business because the exercise of the right was made use of effectually, by banks hostile to the system, to place the Suffolk in a false position before the public.) Yet the bank had not labored in vain : it found the currency of New England in a chaotic state ; but by putting this principle into practice it had brought order out of confusion, and had compelled the banks to keep themselves stronger than they otherwise would, and to live up to a principle the justice of which they could not deny, although the practice of it might cause them to forego some seeming immediate profits: and to this latter cause must be attributed much of the hostility it provoked.

The directors of the Suffolk Bank were not only just in their dealings with the other banks, but were patriotic in the hour of their country's need. On the seventeenth of April, 1861, the day after the Massachusetts regiments of militia left Boston to relieve Washington, then threatened by an invasion from the seceded States, they voted to advance the Governor of the Commonwealth $100,000, " to be used in the pres-

ent emergency, and subject to the future approval of
the Legislature"; also to purchase of the Secretary of
the Treasury, at Washington, a like amount of United
States six per cent. Treasury notes at par. Three
days after, J. Henry Williams, one of the clerks, left
for active duty with the militia of the State, and the
bank presented him with one hundred dollars towards
his outfit.

On the twenty-fourth of July, the bank loaned the
General Government $100,000 for sixty days; and on
the nineteenth of August voted it expedient to take
its proportion of the ten million national loan assigned
to Boston, under the proposed arrangement between
the Secretary of the Treasury and the banks of New
York, Philadelphia, and Boston. On the fifth of October it again subscribed its proportion to a loan of fifty
millions to the Government; on the twentieth of November it took United States twenty-year bonds to
the amount of $300,000; and in September, 1863, it
subscribed $250,000 towards the new loan, being its
full proportion. About this time leave of absence was
granted to Charles L. Holbrook, the book-keeper, who
had been commissioned Colonel of the Forty-third
Massachusetts Regiment of Volunteers. In the case
of four other officers of the bank, who had been
drafted, substitutes were furnished on account of their
valuable services. The directors also voted six months'
back pay to the officers who had served in the army,
and afterwards returned to duty.

In May, 1862, Mr. Grubb died, after having served
the bank as principal officer of the foreign money department for nearly forty years; and the directors
placed on record their appreciation of his services as a

most faithful, able, and judicious officer. He was succeeded by Mr. Eli E. Russell, who had been in the employ of the bank twenty-nine years. Mr. Russell continued in charge of the redemption department till the twenty-fifth of April, 1866, when, the expenses of the department becoming much in excess of its earnings, a committee was appointed " to discontinue the present system of redemption at the earliest practicable moment." Accordingly, the clerks in this department were discharged, and paid to the first of September. Mr. E. E. Russell, the chief, received a grant of one thousand dollars and pay to the first of October, having been in the employ of the bank thirty-three years. Like gratuity and pay were also given to D. H. Belknap and W. B. Sherman, who had been in the department forty years and seventeen years respectively.

CHAPTER VIII.

In June, 1864, the present National Bank Act was passed ; and on the first of January following the bank organized under that Act as the Suffolk National Bank, by which name it is now known. A dividend of $128 per share was paid to the stockholders, in addition to which they received one share in the new national bank for each share held by them in the old bank. At the same time the capital of the new bank was increased from $1,000,000 to $1,500,000, and each stockholder had the privilege of taking one new share for each two shares held before.

On the fifth of May, 1865, Mr. J. Amory Davis, the President, died, and on the twenty-fourth of June Mr. Nathaniel Hooper was elected to fill the vacancy. Mr. Hooper took the position temporarily only, and on the thirty-first of January, 1866, resigned, and Mr. Samuel W. Swett was elected.

The redemption of foreign money being now at an end, the bank turned its attention to the regular business of discounting mercantile paper. It retained the accounts of a large number of New England banks, which had been its correspondents under the old system. On these accounts interest was paid. Its success was marked, till the panic of 1873, having paid an average dividend of nine and three eighths per cent. per annum, and accumulated a surplus of two hundred thousand dollars since its incorporation as a national bank. The panic found it in a strong condition ; and it was able to meet all its liabilities, without being obliged to resort to clearing-house certificates by the pledge of its securities.

Since 1873, by reason of the low rates of interest and the heavy burden of taxes, it has been obliged to reduce its dividends first to eight per cent. and subsequently to six per cent. per annum.

On the thirty-first of January, 1874, Mr. Swett resigned on account of ill health, having served as President just eight years ; and Mr. Henry Austin Whitney was chosen in his place. He occupied the position but two years, when he resigned to take the presidency of the Boston and Providence Railroad. Mr. Swett again held the position temporarily till the first of April, 1876, when the office was filled by the election of the present incumbent.

APPENDIX.

OFFICERS

OF

THE SUFFOLK BANK,

FROM APRIL 1, 1818, TO DECEMBER 31, 1864.

―――――――

PRESIDENTS.

Ebenezer Francis	April,	1818, to April,	1825.
Samuel Hubbard	April,	1825, to November,	1825.
Henry B. Stone	November,	1825, to June,	1849.
Jeffrey Richardson . . .	June,	1849, to April,	1854.
J. Amory Davis	April,	1854, to December,	1864.

CASHIERS.

Matthew S. Parker . . .	April,	1818, to February,	1837.
Isaac C. Brewer	February,	1837, to August,	1853.
Edward Tyler	August,	1853, to December,	1864.

FOREIGN MONEY COMMITTEE.

John Amory Lowell . . .	April,	1825, to January,	1867
Jeffrey Richardson . . .	April,	1825, to January,	1867.
William Lawrence . . .	April,	1825, to October,	1848.
Ebenezer Breed	April,	1825, to October,	1839.
Henry B. Stone	November,	1825, to June,	1849.
William W. Tucker . . .	October,	1847, to November,	1854.
J. Wiley Edmands . . .	October,	1849, to December,	1852.
Samuel Frothingham, Jr. .	October,	1853, to January,	1867.
J. Amory Davis	April,	1854, to May,	1865.
Francis Curtis	October,	1853, to January,	1865.
James S. Amory	January,	1865, to January,	1867.

DIRECTORS

OF

THE SUFFOLK BANK,

FROM APRIL 1, 1818, TO DECEMBER 31, 1864.

————◆————

Ebenezer Breed	. . . .	February,	1818, to October,	1839.
Andrew Ritchie	. . . .	February,	1818, to October,	1818.
Thomas Motley	. . . .	{ February,	1818, to October,	1818.
		October,	1820, to October,	1822.
Samuel Hubbard	. . . .	February,	1818, to March,	1842.
John W. Boott	. . . .	{ February,	1818, to October,	1820.
		April,	1822, to October,	1822.
		January	1826, to October,	1826.
Daniel P. Parker	. . . .	February,	1818, to October,	1822.
William Lawrence	. . . .	February,	1818, to October,	1848.
Eliphalet Williams	. . . .	February,	1818, to October,	1818.
Edmund Munroe	. . . .	February,	1818, to October,	1818.
Patrick T. Jackson	. . .	February,	1818, to October,	1822.
Ebenezer Francis	. . . .	{ February,	1818, to October,	1832.
		October,	1837, to October,	1838.
George Bond	. . . . .	February,	1818, to October,	1837.
William Appleton	. . . .	October,	1818, to October,	1822.
Samuel Appleton	. . . .	October,	1819, to October,	1820.
William Lander	. . . . .	October,	1819, to November,	1825.
Nathaniel P. Russell	. . .	{ October,	1819, to October,	1820.
		April,	1822, to October,	1848.
John Belknap	. . . . .	{ October,	1820, to December,	1825.
		October,	1832, to October,	1854.
Kirk Boott	. . . . . .	October,	1820, to October,	1822.
Joseph Baker	. . . .	April,	1822, to October,	1839.

George Searle	April,	1822, to October,	1822
John Amory Lowell . . .	October,	1822, to December,	1864.
Nathan Appleton	October,	1822, to January,	1823.
Aaron Baldwin	October,	1822, to October,	1823.
Jeffrey Richardson . .	January,	1823, to December,	1864.
James Means	October,	1823, to October,	1842.
Henry B. Stone.	November, 1825, to June,		1849.
Benjamin R. Nichols . . .	October,	1826, to October,	1848.
Amos A. Lawrence . . .	October,	1838, to October,	1855.
Joseph Balch	October,	1839, to October,	1850.
Ebenezer Chadwick . . .	October,	1841, to October,	1852.
J. Wiley Edmands	{ October,	1842, to December,	1852.
	{ November, 1855, to December,		1864.
William W. Tucker . . .	{ October,	1843, to October,	1855.
	{ November, 1856, to December,		1864.
William Gray	October,	1848, to May,	1852.
Nathaniel Hooper	October,	1848, to December,	1864.
Edward D. Peters	October,	1848, to October,	1856.
Edward Austin	{ October,	1849, to May,	1852.
	{ November, 1854, to December,		1864.
Francis Curtis	May,	1852, to October,	1864.
Samuel Frothingham, Jr. .	May,	1852, to December,	1864.
Charles Amory	October,	1852, to December,	1864.
Thomas A. Goddard . . .	November, 1853, to December,		1864.
J. Amory Davis.	February,	1854, to December,	1864.
Francis B. Crowninshield .	November, 1856, to December,		1864.
James S. Amory	November, 1864, to December,		1864.
Samuel W. Swett	November, 1864, to December,		1864.

DIVIDENDS

OF

THE SUFFOLK BANK,

FROM APRIL, 1, 1818, TO DECEMBER 31, 1864.

1818.		October, $1\frac{1}{2}$ per cent. $= 1\frac{1}{2}$ per cent.
1819.	April, $3\frac{1}{2}$ per cent.	October, $3\frac{1}{2}$ per cent. $= 7$ per cent.
1820.	April, $3\frac{1}{2}$ per cent.	October, $3\frac{1}{2}$ per cent. $= 7$ per cent.
1821.	April, $2\frac{1}{2}$ per cent.	October, 3 per cent. $= 5\frac{1}{2}$ per cent.
1822.	April, $2\frac{1}{2}$ per cent.	October, $2\frac{1}{2}$ per cent. $= 5$ per cent.
1823.	April, $2\frac{1}{2}$ per cent.	October, $2\frac{1}{2}$ per cent. $= 5$ per cent.
1824.	April, $2\frac{1}{2}$ per cent.	October, $2\frac{3}{4}$ per cent. $= 5\frac{1}{4}$ per cent.
1825.	April, 3 per cent.	October, $2\frac{1}{2}$ per cent. $= 5\frac{1}{2}$ per cent.
1826.	April, $2\frac{1}{2}$ per cent.	October, 3 per cent. $= 5\frac{1}{2}$ per cent.
1827.	April, 3 per cent.	October, 3 per cent. $= 6$ per cent.
1828.	April, 3 per cent.	October, 3 per cent. $= 6$ per cent.
1829.	April, 3 per cent.	October, 3 per cent. $= 6$ per cent.
1830.	April, 3 per cent.	October, 3 per cent. $= 6$ per cent.
1831.	April, 3 per cent.	October, 3 per cent. $= 6$ per cent.
1832.	April, 3 per cent.	October, 3 per cent. $= 6$ per cent.
1833.	April, 3 per cent.	October, $3\frac{1}{2}$ per cent. $= 6\frac{1}{2}$ per cent.
1834.	April, 4 per cent.	October, 4 per cent. $= 8$ per cent.
1835.	April, 4 per cent.	October, 4 per cent. $= 8$ per cent.
1836.	April, 4 per cent.	October, 5 per cent. $= 9$ per cent.
1837.	April, 5 per cent.	October, 4 per cent. $= 9$ per cent.
1838.	April, 4 per cent.	October, 5 per cent. $= 9$ per cent.
1839.	April, 5 per cent.	October, 3 per cent. $= 8$ per cent.
1839.	September, extra dividend, $33\frac{1}{3}$ per cent.	
1840.	April, 4 per cent.	October, 4 per cent. $= 8$ per cent.

1841.	April, 4	per cent.	October, 4	per cent.	=	8	per cent.
1842.	April, 4	per cent.	October, 4	per cent.	=	8	per cent.
1843.	April, 4	per cent.	October, 4	per cent.	=	8	per cent.
1844.	April, 4	per cent.	October, 4	per cent.	=	8	per cent.
1845.	April, 4	per cent.	October, 4	per cent.	=	8	per cent.
1846.	April, 4	per cent.	October, 4	per cent.	=	8	per cent.
1847.	April, 5	per cent.	October, 5	per cent.	=	10	per cent.
1848.	April, 5	per cent.	October, 5	per cent.	=	10	per cent.
1849.	April, 5	per cent.	October, 5	per cent.	=	10	per cent.
1850.	April, 5	per cent.	October, 5	per cent.	=	10	per cent.
1851.	April, 5	per cent.	October, 5	per cent.	=	10	per cent.
1852.	April, 5	per cent.	October, 5	per cent.	=	10	per cent.
1853.	April, 5	per cent.	October, 5	per cent.	=	10	per cent.
1854.	April, 5	per cent.	October, 5	per cent.	=	10	per cent.
1855.	April, 5	per cent.	October, 5	per cent.	=	10	per cent.
1856.	April, 5	per cent.	October, 5	per cent.	=	10	per cent.
1857.	April, 5	per cent.	October, 5	per cent.	=	10	per cent.
1858.	April, 5	per cent.	October, 5	per cent.	=	10	per cent.
1859.	April, 5	per cent.	October, 4	per cent.	=	9	per cent.
1860.	April, 4½	per cent.	October, 4½	per cent.	=	9	per cent.
1861.	April, 4½	per cent.	October, 4½	per cent.	=	9	per cent.
1862.	April, 4½	per cent.	October, 5	per cent.	=	9½	per cent.
1863.	April, 5	per cent.	October, 5	per cent.	=	10	per cent.
1864.	April, 5	per cent.	October, 5	per cent.	=	10	per cent.
1865.	January, 128 per cent.						

Average 11½ per cent. per annum; or $8\frac{3}{100}$ per cent. per annum
and two extra dividends amounting to $161\frac{33}{100}$ per cent.

OFFICERS

OF

THE SUFFOLK NATIONAL BANK,

FROM JANUARY 1, 1865, TO JANUARY 1, 1878.

PRESIDENTS.

J. Amory Davis	January,	1865, to May,	1865.
Nathaniel Hooper	June,	1865, to January, 1866.	
Samuel W. Swett . . . . {	January,	1866, to January, 1874.	
	January,	1876, to April,	1876.
Henry Austin Whitney . .	February,	1874, to January, 1876.	
David R. Whitney	April,	1876, to present time.	

CASHIER.

Edward Tyler . . . . . . January, 1865, to present time.

DIRECTORS.

John Amory Lowell	January,	1865, to present time.
Jeffrey Richardson.	January,	1865, to present time.
J. Wiley Edmands.	January,	1865, to January, 1877.
William W. Tucker	January,	1865, to present time.
Nathaniel Hooper	January,	1865, to present time.
Edward Austin	January,	1865, to present time.
Samuel Frothingham, Jr. . .	January,	1865, to January, 1873.
Charles Amory	January,	1865, to January, 1866.
Thomas A. Goddard	January,	1865, to January, 1869.
J. Amory Davis	January,	1865, to May, 1865.
Francis B. Crowninshield . .	January,	1865, to May, 1877.

James S. Amory . . . . . January, 1865, to present time.
Samuel W. Swett . . . . . January, 1865, to present time.
Henry Austin Whitney . . . February, 1874, to present time.
Charles H. Dalton . . . . . January, 1876, to present time.
David R. Whitney . . . . . April, 1876, to present time.
A. Lawrence Edmands . . . Elected January, 1878.

10

DIVIDENDS

OF

THE SUFFOLK NATIONAL BANK,

FROM JANUARY 1, 1865, TO JANUARY 1, 1878.

1865.		October, 5 per cent. = 5 per cent.
1866.	April, 4 per cent.	October, 4 per cent. = 8 per cent.
1867.	April, 4 per cent.	October, 4 per cent. = 8 per cent.
1868.	April, 4 per cent.	October, 5 per cent. = 9 per cent.
1869.	April, 5 per cent.	October, 5 per cent. = 10 per cent.
1870.	April, 5 per cent.	October, 5 per cent. = 10 per cent.
1871.	April, 5 per cent.	October, 5 per cent. = 10 per cent.
1872.	April, 5 per cent.	October, 5 per cent. = 10 per cent.
1873.	April, 5 per cent.	October, 5 per cent. = 10 per cent.
1874.	April, 4 per cent.	October, 4 per cent. = 8 per cent.
1875.	April, 4 per cent.	October, 4 per cent. = 8 per cent.
1876.	April, 3 per cent.	October, 3 per cent. = 6 per cent.
1877.	April, 3 per cent.	October, 3 per cent. = 6 per cent.

Average $8\frac{30}{100}$ per cent. per annum.

OFFICERS

OF

THE SUFFOLK NATIONAL BANK,

JANUARY 1, 1878.

———◆———

RECORD OF THEIR SERVICES.

David R. Whitney .	President,	1 year, 9 months.
Edward Tyler . {	Cashier,	24 years, 4 months.
	Book-keeper and Clerk,	15 years, 6 months.

DIRECTORS.

John Amory Lowell . {	Director,	55 years, 2 mos.
	Foreign Money Com.,	41 years, 9 mos.
Jeffrey Richardson . {	Director,	54 years, 11 mos.
	President,	4 years, 10 mos.
	Foreign Money Com.,	41 years 9 mos.
William W. Tucker . {	Director,	33 years, 1 mo.
	Foreign Money Com.,	7 years, 1 mo.
Nathaniel Hooper . . {	Director,	29 years, 2 mos. .
	President,	7 mos.
Edward Austin . . .	Director,	25 years, 8 mos.
James S. Amory . . . {	Director,	13 years, 1 mo.
	Foreign Money Com.,	2 years.
Samuel W. Swett . . {	Director,	13 years, 1 mo.
	President,	8 years, 3 mos.
Henry Austin Whitney. {	Director,	3 years, 10 mos.
	President,	1 year, 11 mos.
Charles H. Dalton .	Director,	2 years.